It's not just "embroidery"

It's Primitive Embroidery. And it's the greatest thing to happen to needle art in decades.

These fresh designs by artist Jennie Baer are all about getting
you into the world of fabric art—fast! Follow the simple directions to
transfer a pattern onto fabric, then use basic stitches and easy
embellishments to finish textile beauty that's very new, very you.

While we're at it, why don't we make your creative experience even sweeter?
We're including three different sizes for each of these 12 designs, so you don't
have to worry about enlarging or reducing them for your project. Just "choose
and use." To see which size patterns were used for the photography models,
check the supply lists included with the projects. The key to creating
modern/primitive art is truly in your hands!

BOUT THE DESIGNER

**For Jennie Baer,
designing is all about
being open to new ideas.**

"I've been an artist for as long as
an remember," says the Illinois
sident, "however, I've only been
signing embroidery patterns for
out two years now. That started
en I saw a friend embroidering a
mitive pattern, and I thought 'I
n do that.' So I started making
 own patterns."

Jennie's creative nature is a family
ait. Her father writes science
tion novels, while her mother
signs quilts. Jennie's creative

outlet is drawing, and most of her
patterns are fashioned using this
traditional method. Yet she's also
been known to start with an oil
painting in order to arrive at her
final design.

"I've found that anything can be a
primitive embroidery pattern. That's
because anything can translate
into a simple line drawing. I've also
learned that you must not be hard
on yourself about your work as an
artist or as an embroiderer. You
can't predict what will turn out best,
and sometimes the design that
pleased you the least is the one
that everyone else loves."

Jennie's biggest fans may be her
husband and two-year-old son, but
they are gaining more rivals for the
title every day.

"As my designs began to accumulate,
I created Homeberries.com as a
place to share them with a larger
audience. It's been fun to see how
the 'Prim' trend is exploding. It's
everywhere. Once my Website was up
and running, I realized it was time to
contact Leisure Arts to see if they
would be interested in publishing
some of my designs."

And the rest, as they say, is
Primitive history.

For digital downloads of Leisure Arts'
best-selling designs,
visit **leisureartslibrary.com**.

Snow Birds

What you need
Large pattern, pg. 3 (alternate sizes, pg. 23)
Tissue paper
Embroidery floss, pearl cotton, and beads (see Key—
 we used floss except where noted)
Black linen (we used a 13$\frac{1}{2}$" x 14$\frac{1}{2}$" piece)
Frame (ours has a 9" x 9$\frac{3}{4}$" opening)

What to do
Start with Embroidery Basics (pg. 35). Transfer the pattern (the Tissue Paper method works best for this one) and embroider the design onto the linen. Add a bead to the center of each snowflake. Finish the stitched piece—we centered ours in a whitewashed wooden frame.

KEY

Satin Stitch
- ▪ DMC 347 – 3 strands

Straight Stitch
- —— DMC blanc – 2 strands
- —— DMC blanc #3 pearl cotton
- —— DMC blanc #12 pearl cotton
- —— DMC 347 – 3 strands

Backstitch
- – – – DMC blanc – 2 strands
- – – – DMC blanc #3 pearl cotton
- – – – DMC blanc #5 pearl cotton

French Knot
- • DMC blanc #5 pearl cotton
- · DMC blanc – 1 strand

Bead
- ● 02058 Mill Hill Seed Bead

Picture The Positive

What you need

Large pattern, pg. 5
   (alternate sizes, pg. 24)
Tissue paper
Linen embroidery floss
   (see Key)
Pre-finished linen
   placemat (ours has an
   8" x 13" stitching area)
Fabric strip for hanging
   sleeve (ours is 2¼"
   wide by the width of
   the placemat)

What to do

Start with Embroidery
Basics (pg. 35).
Transfer the pattern
and embroider the
design (we loved the
idea of turning a
placemat into a wall
hanging). To add a
hanging sleeve, just
press the edges of
the fabric strip ½" to
the wrong side and
topstitch. Whipstitch
the long edges of the
hanging sleeve to
the top back of the
placemat.

Sometimes you just have to picture the

Positive

4

Sometimes You
just have to picture the

Positive

Be Thou Humble

What you need

Large pattern, pg. 7 (alternate sizes, pg. 25)
Tissue paper
Cream linen (we cut an 8$\frac{1}{2}$" x 11$\frac{1}{4}$" piece)
Embroidery floss (see Key)
Background fabric (we used a 12" x 14" gingham piece)
Frame (ours has a 7$\frac{3}{4}$" x 9$\frac{3}{4}$" opening)

What to do

Start with Embroidery Basics (pg. 35). Transfer the pattern onto the linen piece (at this point, we omitted the running stitch outline and the wording). Embroider the design. To finish your piece like we did, trim the linen piece to 4$\frac{1}{2}$" x 7$\frac{1}{4}$", and then center and stitch the piece on background fabric with a freehand running stitch. Next, transfer and stitch the wording to the background. Pull threads from the linen piece to fringe before framing.

Be Thou Humble

KEY

Satin Stitch – 3 strands
DMC 3831

Stem Stitch – 3 strands
DMC 3052

Running Stitch – 3 strands
DMC 938

Straight Stitch – 3 strands
DMC 3052

Backstitch – 3 strands
DMC 938

French Knot – 2 strands
• DMC 3853

Lazy Daisy – 3 strands
DMC 3052*
DMC 3855

* For a more primitive look, make open-ended Lazy Daisy leaves.

All Is Well

What you need

Medium pattern, pg. 26 (alternate sizes, pgs. 9 and 26)
Tissue paper
Embroidery floss (see Key)
Hand-dyed wool (ours measures 12" x 14")
Frame (ours has a 7½" x 9¼" opening)

What to do

Start with Embroidery Basics (pg. 35). Transfer the pattern (use the Tissue Paper method with wool) and embroider the design. In contrast to the coarse wool, we used all six strands of floss on most of the design to add sheen to the stitching. Finish the piece as you like—we chose a simple, textured frame.

KEY

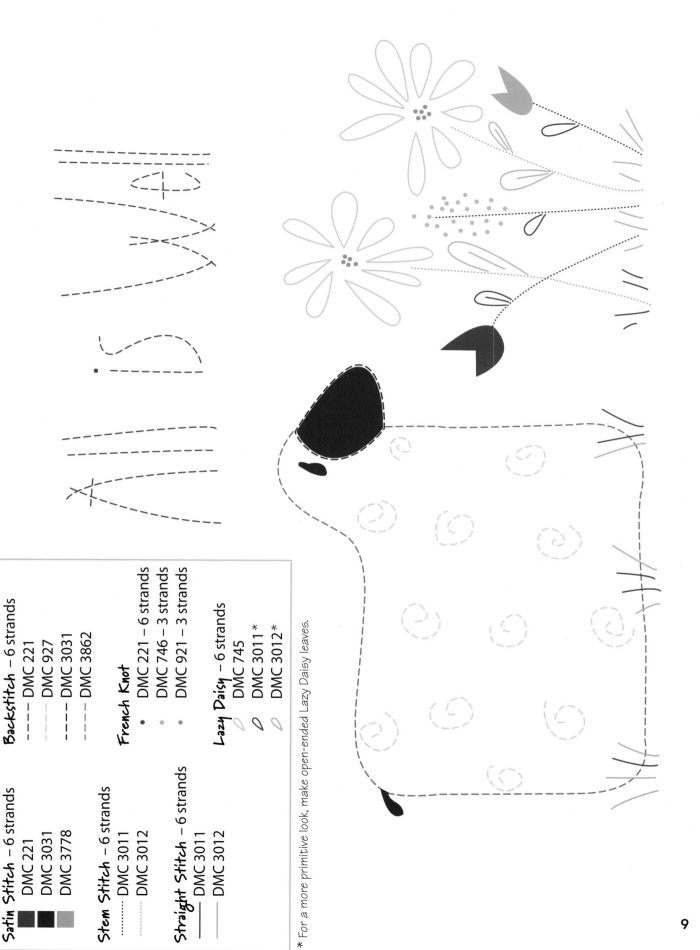

Satin Stitch – 6 strands
- ■ DMC 221
- ■ DMC 3031
- ■ DMC 3778

Stem Stitch – 6 strands
- ⋯⋯ DMC 3011
- ⋯⋯ DMC 3012

Straight Stitch – 6 strands
- —— DMC 3011
- —— DMC 3012

Backstitch – 6 strands
- – – – DMC 221
- – – – DMC 927
- – – – DMC 3031
- – – – DMC 3862

French Knot
- ● DMC 221 – 6 strands
- ● DMC 746 – 3 strands
- ● DMC 921 – 3 strands

Lazy Daisy – 6 strands
- ⊘ DMC 745
- ⊘ DMC 3011 *
- ⊘ DMC 3012 *

* For a more primitive look, make open-ended Lazy Daisy leaves.

9

Welcome Friends

What you need

Medium pattern, pg. 27 (alternate sizes, pgs. 11 and 27)
Tissue paper
Embroidery floss (see Key—use one floss color as we
   did, or experiment with several to fit your color scheme)
Brown fabric (we cut two 12" x 18½" pieces for the pillow
   front and back)
Polyester fiberfill

What to do

Start with Embroidery Basics (pg. 35). Transfer
the pattern and embroider the design on the fabric
(we omitted the wording from ours). To make a pillow,
match the right sides of the fabric pieces. Beginning
at the bottom and leaving an opening for turning, sew
the pieces together. Trim the corners and turn the
pillow right side out. Stuff and sew the opening closed.

KEY

Satin Stitch – 3 strands
DMC 3845

Running Stitch – 2 strands
— — DMC 3845

Backstitch – 3 strands
‑‑‑‑ DMC 3845

French Knot – 2 strands
• DMC 3845

Lazy Daisy – 3 strands
DMC 3845

Flower In Disguise

What you need

Large pattern, pg. 13 (alternate sizes, pg. 28)
Tissue paper
White linen (we cut a 13" x 16" piece)
Embroidery floss (see Key)
Assorted buttons (optional)
Frame (ours has an 8" x 11¼" opening)

What to do

Start with Embroidery Basics (pg. 35) before beginning Transfer the pattern onto the linen piece (we omitted some design elements and substituted buttons for others). Embroider the design, adding buttons as you wish. Finish the stitched piece—we placed ours in a shopworn wood frame.

KEY

Satin Stitch
– 3 strands

DMC 304
DMC 838
DMC 976
DMC 3826

Stem Stitch
·········· DMC 838
– 3 strands

Straight Stitch
——— DMC 3362
– 2 strands

Backstitch
– – – DMC 304
– 3 strands
– – – DMC 815
– 3 strands
– – – DMC 3362
– 2 strands
– – – DMC 3364
– 2 strands

French Knot
• DMC 304
– 3 strands
• DMC 728
– 2 strands
• DMC 815
– 3 strands

Lazy Daisy
DMC 976
– 3 strands
DMC 3362
– 2 strands
DMC 3826
– 3 strands

A weed is no more than a flower in Disguise

13

Each Day

What you need

Large pattern, pg. 15
  (alternate sizes, pg. 29)
Tissue paper
Embroidery floss (see Key)
Cream linen (we cut a
  9½" x 15" piece)
Blue colored pencil
  (optional)
Frame (ours has a
  5¼" x 10½" opening)

What to do

Start with Embroidery
Basics (pg. 35). Transfer
the pattern and
embroider the design on
the linen piece. To soften
the look, we lightly shaded
the jar with a blue pencil
(to add shading to yours,
first practice on a linen
scrap until you get the
hang of it). Finish the
stitched piece—we liked
the simplicity of this
red frame.

Winter Berry

What you need

Large pattern, pg. 17 (alternate sizes, pg. 30)

Tissue paper

Embroidery floss (see Key)

Tea towel (large enough to wrap around a pillow form with some extra on the sides—ours is 20" x 29" and has a 6" wide center stripe)

Pillow form (ours measures 12" x 16")

Buttons (we chose six 1¹⁄₈" dia. white buttons)

What to do

Start with Embroidery Basics (pg. 35). It's simple to turn a towel into a pillow—just wrap the towel around your pillow form and trim the short ends, leaving a 1" overlap (we trimmed our towel to 20" x 25"). Center and transfer the pattern on the bottom half of the towel and embroider the design. Matching right sides and using a ½" seam allowance, sew the raw edges together. Turn the pillow right side out and insert the pillow form. Sew buttons on each end.

KEY

Satin Stitch – 3 strands
- DMC ecru
- DMC 3371

Running Stitch – 2 strands
- — — DMC 3371

Straight Stitch – 2 strands
- —— DMC 3371

Backstitch
- – – – DMC ecru – 2 strands
- – – – DMC 3371 – 3 strands

French Knot
- • DMC 3371 – 2 strands
- • DMC 3371 – 3 strands

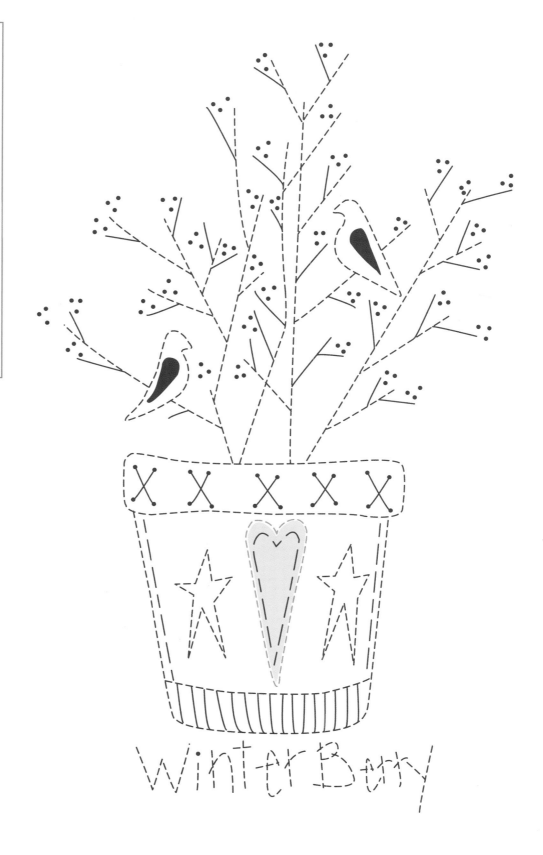

17

Spring, Summer, Autumn, and Winter

What you need
Small patterns, pgs. 31–34 (alternate sizes, pgs. 19–22 and 31–34)
Tissue paper
Variegated embroidery floss (see Keys)
Cotton tea towels (ours are 28" x 29")

What to do
Start with Embroidery Basics (pg. 35). Transfer each pattern and embroider the design (we centered ours 2" from the bottom of the towel and used variegated floss to make each piece unique). These designs make great framed pieces, too.

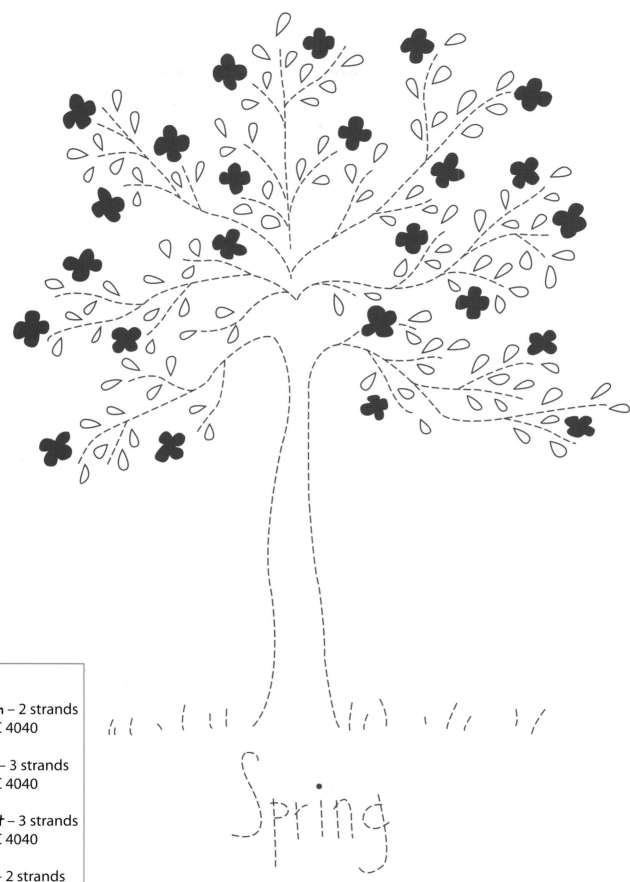

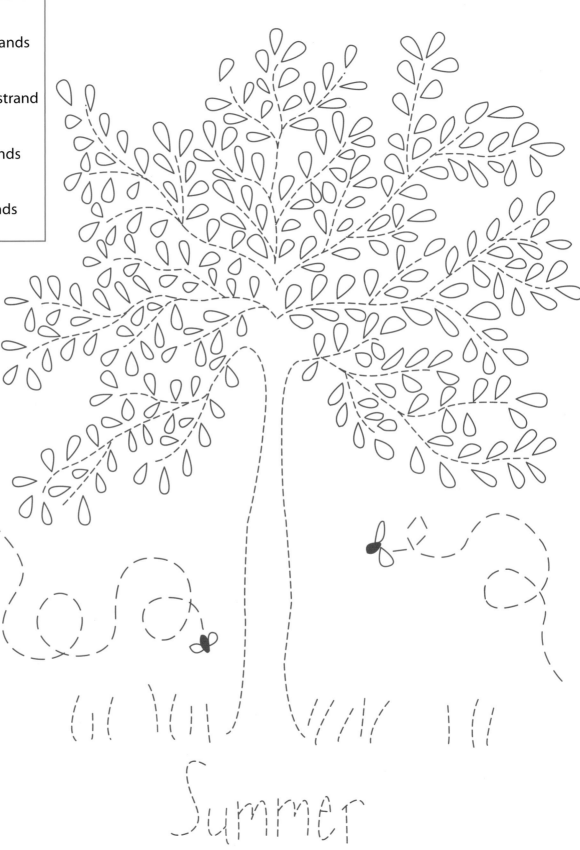

KEY

Backstitch – 3 strands
- - - DMC 4090

Lazy Daisy – 2 strands
⬮ DMC 4090

Autumn

21

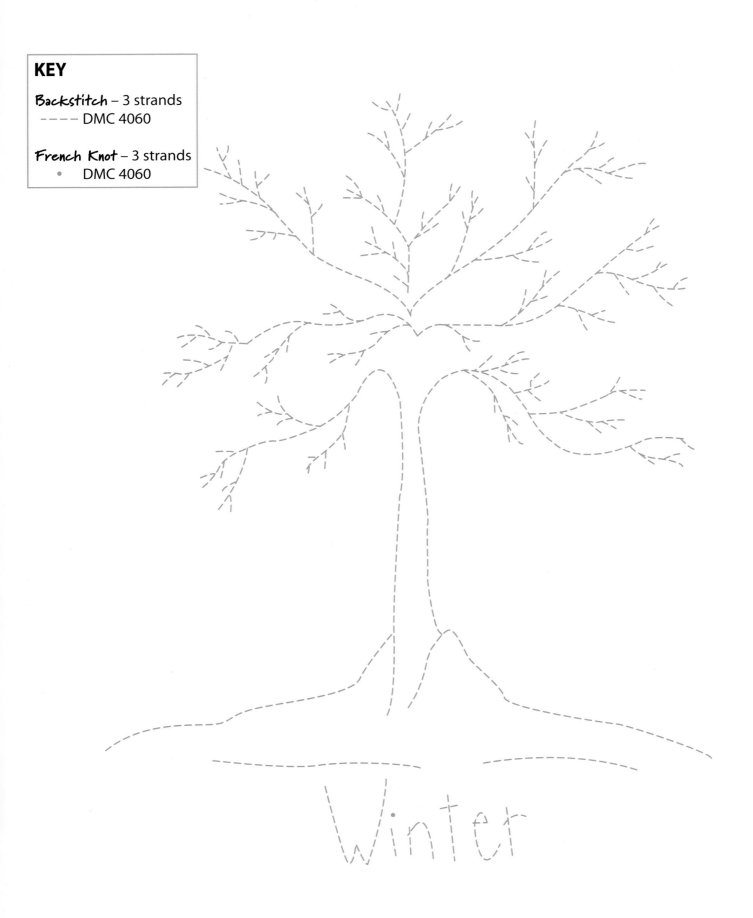

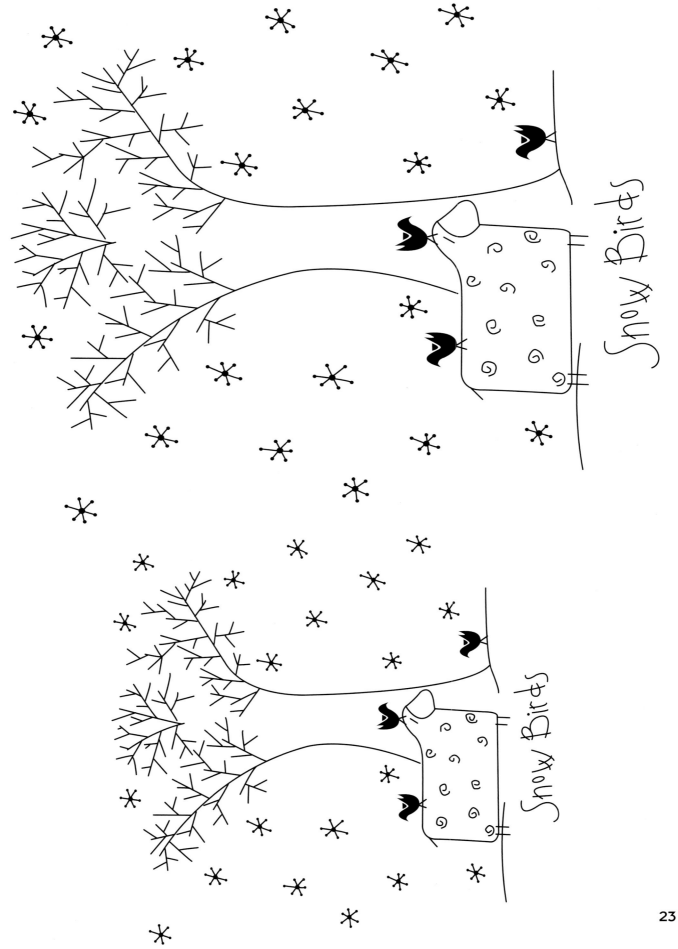

Snow Birds

Snow Birds

Sometimes You
just have to picture the

Positive

Sometimes You
just have to picture the

Positive

Be Thou Humble

Be Thou Humble

All is Well

All is Well

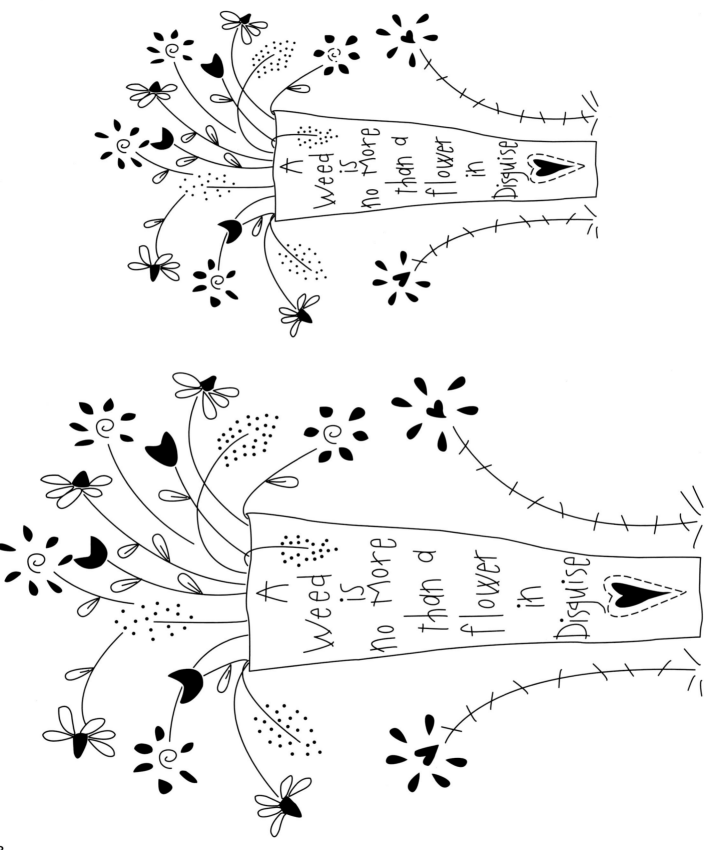

28

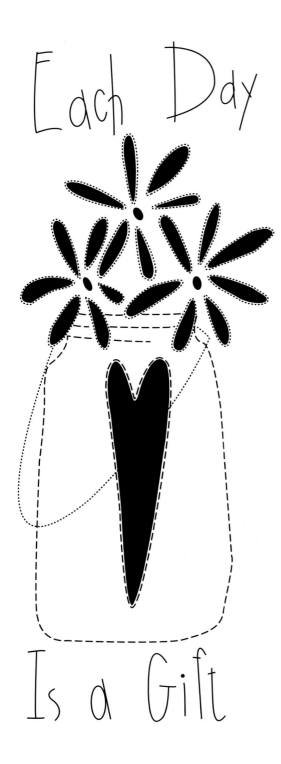

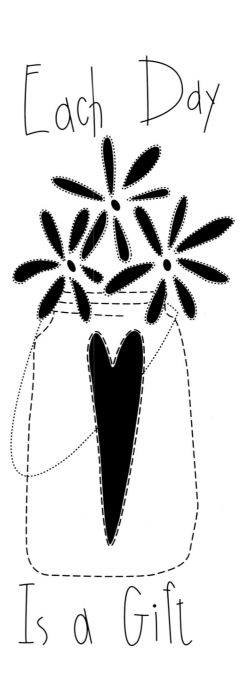

30

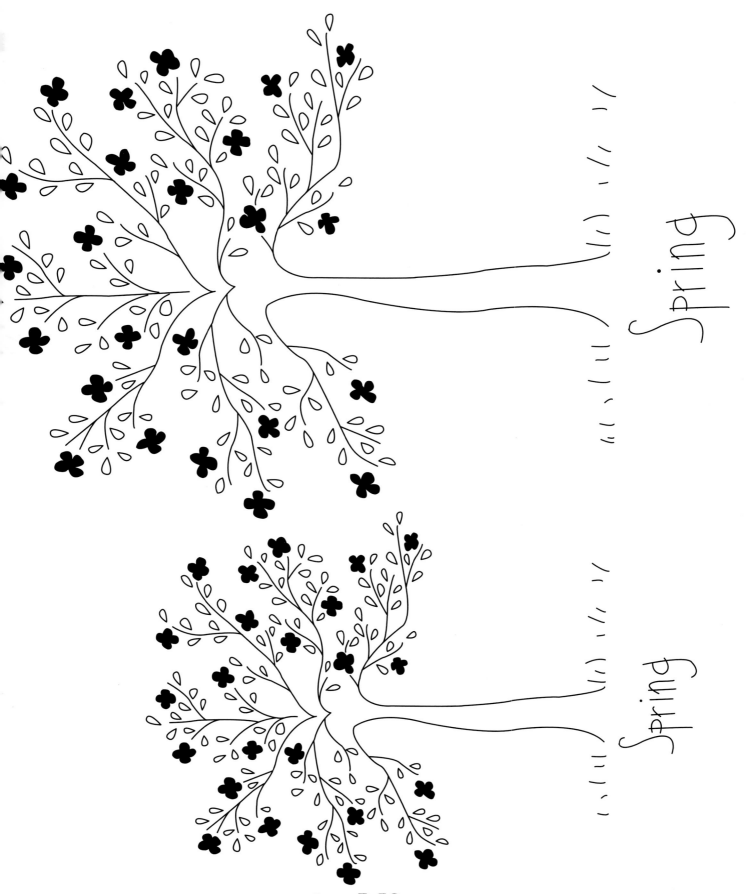

Spring

Spring

SPRING

Summer

Summer

32

AUTUMN

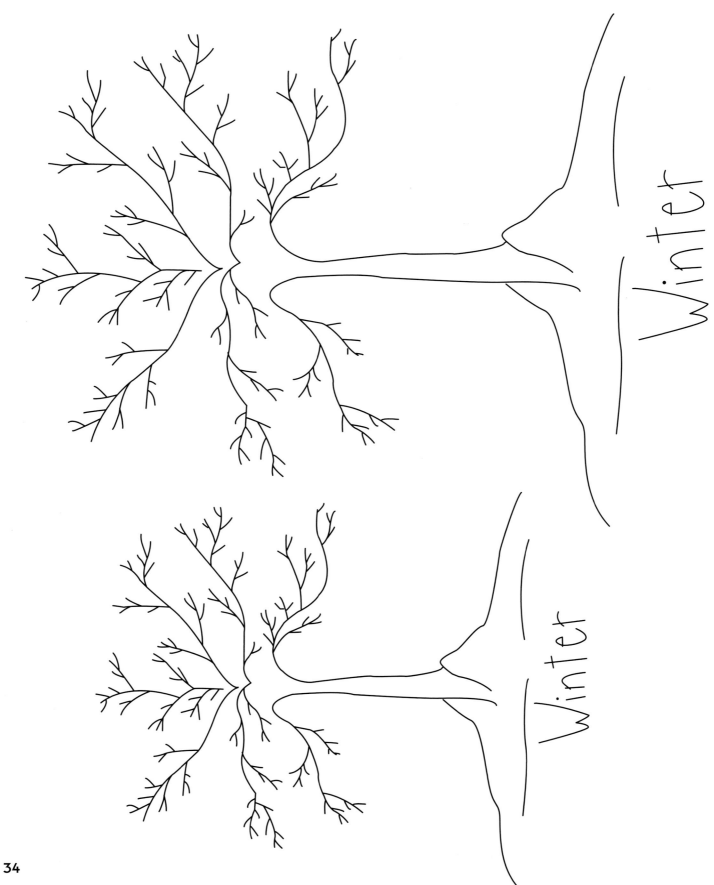

Winter

Winter

EMBROIDERY BASICS

TRANSFERRING THE PATTERNS

There are different ways to transfer patterns to fabric. Use the method that works best with the design and fabric you've chosen. See a demo webcast of Transferring Methods at leisurearts.com.

Tissue Paper Method

For wool, felt, or dark fabric, trace the pattern onto tissue paper and pin it to the fabric. Embroider the design, stitching through the tissue paper. Carefully tear away the tissue paper and add any beads or other embellishments.

Water-soluble Pen Method

For sheer fabric, trace the pattern onto tissue paper and place it under the fabric. Trace the lines with a water-soluble pen (or for fine details, use a sharp colored pencil). Can't see through the fabric? Tape the tissue pattern and the fabric to a sunny window or light box. Trace the pattern and you're ready to stitch. Lightly spritz the finished design with water to remove any visible pen markings.

ADDING BEADS

To attach beads, use one strand of floss and a fine needle that will pass through the bead. Knot the floss and bring the needle up from the back of the fabric. Run the needle through the bead and back down through the fabric. Knot the floss close to the back of the fabric.

EMBROIDERY STITCHES

Follow the stitch diagrams to bring the needle up at odd numbers and down at even numbers.

BACKSTITCH
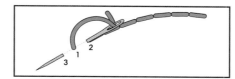

LAZY DAISY
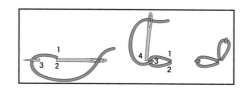

RUNNING STITCH
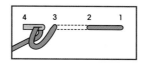

STEM STITCH

FRENCH KNOT
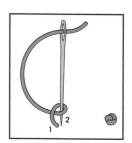

SATIN STITCH
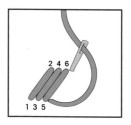

STRAIGHT STITCH
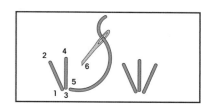

35

Explore your inner artist!

Sure **fabric art** is hot—but what if you don't consider yourself to be an **artist**? What if you can't even draw a **straight line**?

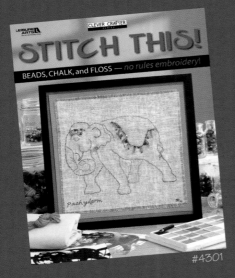

#4301

This **new technique** allows you to create **original textile art** that begins with your favorite **photograph** or **pattern**!

We will show you how to **trace** and **transfer** the key lines of your design onto fabric and then use **simple embroidery stitches** to bring it to life. Then you can **embellish** your art with fabric, beads, chalk—**anything you like!**

For more embroidery inspiration, sign up for our free e-newsletter at leisurearts.com and receive free projects, reviews of our newest books, handy tips and more.

Visit your favorite retailer, or shop online at theleisureboutique.com. Have questions? Call us at 1.800.526.5111.

the art of everyday living

Production Team

Design Adaptation
Kathy Middleton Elrod

Technical Writer
Laura Siar Holyfield

Editorial Writer
Susan McManus Johnson

Production Artist
Angela Ormsby Stark

Photography Stylist
Sondra Daniel